to

from

To Amelia, Harriet, Lucie

and Jay—A.A.

Text copyright © Lois Rock
Illustrations copyright © Alex Ayliffe

Original edition published in English under the title *My Very First Bible* by Lion Hudson plc, Oxford, England. This edition copyright © 2015 Lion Hudson.

North American edition entitled *My Very First Bible* published by Good Books, 2016, 2021

Good Books books may be purchased in bulk at special discounts for sales promotion, corporate gifts, fund-raising, or educational purposes. Special editions can also be created to specifications. For details, contact the Special Sales Department, Good Books, 307 West 36th Street, 11th Floor, New York, NY 10018 or info@skyhorsepublishing.com.

Good Books is an imprint of Skyhorse Publishing, Inc.®, a Delaware corporation.

Visit our website at www.goodbooks.com.

10 9 8 7 6 5 4 3 2 1

Manufactured in China, December 2021
This product conforms to CPSIA 2008

Library of Congress Cataloging-in-Publication Data is available on file.

Cover design by Sarah Brody
Cover illustration credit Alex Ayliffe

Print ISBN: 978-1-68099-754-5
Ebook ISBN: 978-1-68099-164-2

my very first
Bible

Words by
Lois Rock

Pictures by
Alex Ayliffe

Good Books

Contents

Old Testament

New Testament

Dear God,
These are Bible stories.
Help me to listen.

Dear God,
These are Bible stories.
Help me to imagine.

Dear God,
These are Bible stories.
Help me to understand.

Old Testament

In the
Beginning

Think of the dark.
Make it darker.
Think of the darkest
dark.

In the beginning,
there was nothing but
dark.

Then God spoke:
"Let there be light."

And the very first light shone
brightly.

God spread the sky wide above the ocean, and folded the land to make hills and valleys.

God covered the earth with plants: grasses and flowers, vegetables and trees.

The sun shone in the daytime,
and the moon and stars waited
for their turn in the night-time.

God made all the creatures.

Birds flew in the sky.

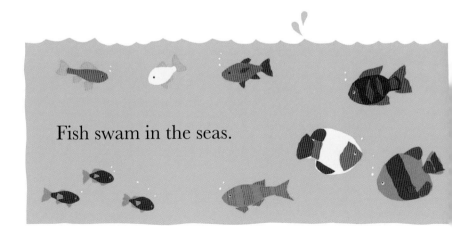

Fish swam in the seas.

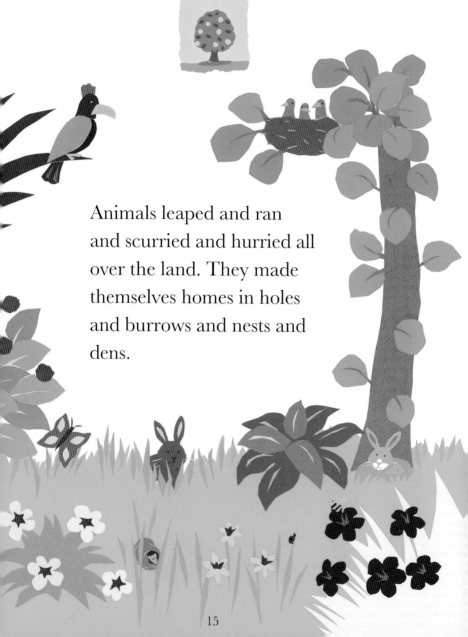

Animals leaped and ran
and scurried and hurried all
over the land. They made
themselves homes in holes
and burrows and nests and
dens.

Then God made people—man and woman. "Welcome," said God. "You are my friends, and I want you to be safe and happy. Take care of the good world I have made for you.

"Never choose to know about
bad things: they will only
make you sad."

Everything was perfect…

Then, one day, people wanted
to find out about bad things as
well as good things.

The snake whispered what to do:
they ate some fruit God had told
them not to eat.

Their world changed.

They were no longer good
friends with God.

Instead, they felt all alone
in an unkind world.
They had to work very
hard for everything they
needed.

"Can things ever be put right again?"
they wondered. People have been
wondering ever since.

Noah and the Ark

Long ago, God looked down to see the world.

God had made a good world. Now people were spoiling it.

They were always fighting.

"I'm sorry I ever made the world," said God. "I shall wash it away."

God saw that there was
one good man: Noah.

"I want you to build a
big boat," said God to
Noah. "It will be called
the ark."

Noah was puzzled.

"There is going to be a flood," said God.
"You must take your family on the ark,
to keep them safe."

Noah began to build.

God said, "Noah, you must also take animals onto the ark. You must take a father and a mother of every kind of animal."

Noah and his family were very
busy doing as God wanted.

Then it rained and rained.
The whole world was flooded.

The ark floated on the flood
water for days and days and days.

At last, the rain stopped.
The water started to go down.

Bump! Noah's ark hit the top
of a mountain and got stuck
there.

Noah let out a raven.
It flew and flew and
kept on flying.

Noah let out a dove.
The first time, it soon
flew back.

The second time, it came back
with an olive branch in its
beak. The third time, it flew
away.

"It must have found land,"
said Noah.

Soon the land was dry. Noah let everyone out of the ark. The animals hurried away to make new homes.

"Thank you, God, for keeping us safe," said Noah.

God was pleased. "Look," said God, "there is my rainbow in the sky. It is a promise that I will keep the whole world safe forever."

Grandfather Abraham

Long ago lived a man named Abram. His family was very rich.

They had sheep and goats and
cattle and donkeys and camels.

One day, God
spoke to Abram.

"Abram, I want you to leave your father's home and go to a new land.

"I have chosen you to be the great-great-great-grandfather of many people. You and your family will bring my blessing to all the world."

Abram believed that what God
said was true. He set out at once
with his wife, Sarai, his family and
his animals.

They reached the land
of Canaan. "You can make your
home here," said God.

It was a good land, but Abram
had to find grass for his animals.

They had to keep on moving from place to place. Life was often hard. Sometimes it made them sad.

"I wonder if what God said is really true," thought Abram.

One dark night, God spoke to Abram
again. "Look up at the stars in the sky…
too many to count," said God. "You will
be the great-great-great- grandfather of
many people… too many to count."

Abram believed that what God said
was true.

"I am going to give you and Sarai new names," said God. "You will be Abraham: Great-great-great-grandfather Abraham.

"Your wife will be Sarah: Great-great-great-grandmother Sarah."

Many years passed. Abraham and Sarah still had no children.

Abraham sighed. "Can I still believe that what God said will come true?" he said.

Sarah looked at other people's children and sighed. "I find it hard to believe that what God said is true," she said.

Then, at last, Sarah and Abraham had a baby. They called him Isaac.

"God has made me so happy I can laugh again," said Sarah. And she knew that one day she was going to be the great-great-great-grandmother of many people.

"This is a time to be happy," said Abraham.
"Now we know that what God says is true."

He was sure that one day
he was going to be the great-great-great-
grandfather of many people.

Joseph and His Dream

Joseph was wearing his very best coat.
He was feeling proud.

His great-grandfather was Abraham.

His grandfather was Isaac.

His father was Jacob.

Jacob had given Joseph the wonderful coat.
It was better than anything he had given to
Joseph's older brothers.

Joseph believed he was very, very important.

His older brothers were very, very jealous.

47

One day, the brothers were out looking after their father's goats and sheep. Jacob sent Joseph to check that everything was all right.

The brothers grabbed him. They took his coat. Then they saw some merchants passing nearby. They sold Joseph to the men.

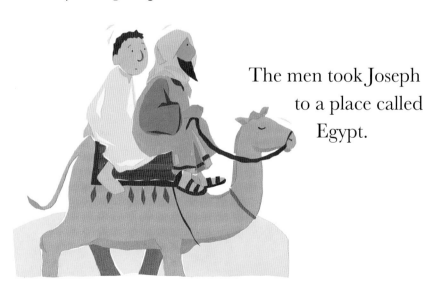

The men took Joseph to a place called Egypt.

The brothers told their father, Jacob, that Joseph was dead. Jacob was very sad.

In Egypt, Joseph was sold as a slave. He had to work very hard. Then someone told a lie about Joseph and he went to prison.

Nobody there cared about Joseph. But God helped Joseph understand dreams and explain their meaning.

One day, the great king of Egypt
had a strange dream. Someone
sent for Joseph.

Joseph understood the king's dream:

"There are going
to be seven years of
good harvests and
seven years of
bad harvests,"
he explained.
"Find someone
wise to keep
grain from the
good harvests; it
will feed the people
when the harvests
are bad."

The king chose Joseph.
He became very rich and very
important.

The bad years came. Joseph was in charge
of using the grain in the barns.

From far away came ten hungry people.

They bowed down to the important man
in charge and asked to buy food.

Joseph knew these people were
his brothers, but they didn't
know who he was.

Was Joseph going to punish
them, or was he going to be
kind?

Joseph really wanted to see his one younger brother, Benjamin. He made the others go to fetch him.

Then, at last, Joseph told the brothers who he was. "God was in charge of everything that happened," he said.
"I was sent to Egypt so that I could rescue you now."

Joseph invited all his family to come
and live in Egypt. There they made
their home.

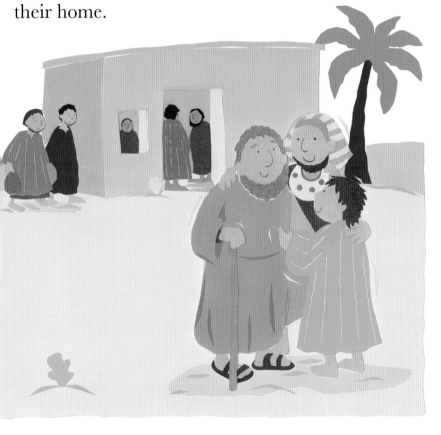

Moses and
the King

When Miriam was a little girl, she liked
to dance and play the
tambourine. She also liked
to listen to stories with her
little brother, Aaron

They liked the story of Great-great-ever-so-many-greats Grandfather Abraham.

"God promised Abraham a land of our own," said Miriam's mother. "Our family came to Egypt many years ago to find food here. Now the king of Egypt has made us slaves.

"Now the king wants our baby boys killed," she sobbed.

"What about my new baby brother?" Miriam asked.

They hid him in a basket among the reeds.

Miriam saw the princess of Egypt
come and find the baby.

"I shall keep him safe," said the princess.
"I shall call him Moses.
But who will take care of him?"

Miriam stepped forward. "I can find
someone to take care of the baby," she said.
She fetched her mother.

When he was older Moses grew up as a prince, but he knew he was one of the slave people.

One day, he got into a bad fight for trying to help a slave, and he had to run away.

He became a shepherd.

In the desert, Moses saw a strange thing: a bush on fire that wasn't burning. He heard God speaking: "Go back to Egypt, Moses, and tell that king to let my people go. Your brother will help you."

Together Moses and Aaron
went to see the king.

"I will not let your
people go," he told
them.

They asked over and over again, but the king always said, "NO!"

"God wants you to let our people go," said Aaron and Moses. "If you don't, there will be trouble."

There was lots of trouble: frogs, then flies, then locusts— everywhere!

There were all sorts of horrible things.

At last, the king told Moses and
Aaron to come and see him.
"Hurry up and go!" he said.

God helped everyone escape.
They set out for the land God had
promised to Great-great-ever-so-many-
greats Grandfather Abraham.

Moses and Aaron led the way.

Miriam played her tambourine and
danced, just like she used to when
she was little.

Brave Joshua

When the way ahead is scary,
who goes first?

Someone who is
strong and brave.

Someone like Joshua.

As Moses led his people to the land God had promised them, he noticed Joshua.

As Moses told the people God's laws, he noticed that Joshua always listened.

"You must love God most of all, and you must love others as you love yourself," said Moses.

Joshua always obeyed and tried to
help others to do the same.

The people wandered for many
years on the way to the new land.
Moses grew old.

He chose Joshua to lead the
people into the new land.
Joshua stood on the bank
of the River Jordan, on the edge
of the new land.

"Teach the people to obey my laws," said God, "and I will help you make the land your home."

The first place the people came to was the city of Jericho. It had walls all around it. Strong soldiers stood on guard.

God told Joshua what to do.

Joshua told the people to march around the city.
One day they marched. Two days they marched.
Three days they marched. Four days they marched.
Five days they marched. Six days they marched.
Seven days they marched, and then…

The priests blew
their trumpets.

All the people
shouted.

The walls of Jericho
fell down.

The people entered the city.

It was the first step towards
making the land a home.

When the land was theirs,
Joshua made sure that
everyone had a share.

Then he asked everyone to come to a great meeting.

"We are at home in the land God has given us," he said. "I have decided that I will always live as God wants: I will love God most of all, and I will love others as much as I love myself. What will you do?"

"We will live as God wants," said the people.

David and His Song

When he was very little, David liked to throw stones.

When he was bigger, he learned to throw them with a sling.

He was good
at throwing—he
could hit what he
wanted.

At night, his mother told him about
God.

She taught him to say
thank-you prayers to God
for everything he had
and for all the things
he could do.

When David was a bit older, his job was looking after the sheep.

He threw stones to scare away wild animals.

David was never scared. He sang thank-you
songs to God for
everything he had and
for all the things he
could do.

One day, David went to visit his big brothers. They were soldiers.

They were fighting fierce enemies.

One was a giant. He wore shiny battle clothes and had a big spear.
"I am Goliath," roared the giant. "If anyone can beat me, then my army will go away! Who dares to try?"

"I dare," said David. For David believed
that God was always with him
and would help him win.

"You're too little,"
said his brothers.

"You're too little,"
said his king.

"But I can fight lions and bears and wolves, and I know God is with me," said David.

"Take care," they warned.

David went out.

He picked up
five stones.

"How dare you fight me
like that!" said the giant.

"I dare because God is with me,"
said David. He put a stone in his
sling.

He threw.

The giant fell.

David grew up to be the next king of his people. He still sang thank-you songs to God for everything he had and for all he could do.

"Dear God, you are my shepherd,
You give me all I need—
My food, my drink, a place to rest,
Yes, you are good indeed.

When all the world seems gloomy
And scary things are near,
You always take good care of me
And so I need not fear.

You've given me so many things,
And everyone can see
The special loving kindness
You always show to me."

Jonah and the Whale

Jonah was feeling grumpy.

"I'm a prophet," he was thinking. "My job is to tell our people about our God—the God who loves us.

"Now God wants me to go and visit our worst enemies—our enemies in Nineveh. And why?

"BECAUSE GOD WANTS TO
FORGIVE THEM FOR ALL THE
BAD THINGS THEY DO!

"Well, I won't."

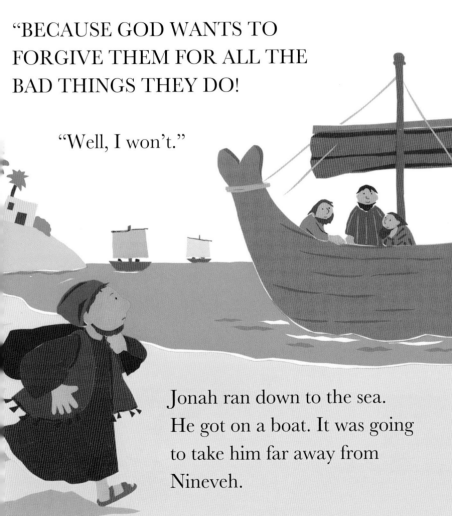

Jonah ran down to the sea.
He got on a boat. It was going
to take him far away from
Nineveh.

Then God sent a storm.

"It's all my fault," wailed Jonah to the sailors. "Throw me overboard, or the storm will sink us all." So they did.

The storm stopped. The sailors on the boat were safe.

Jonah sank deep down in the sea,
where a great big fish came and
swallowed him up.

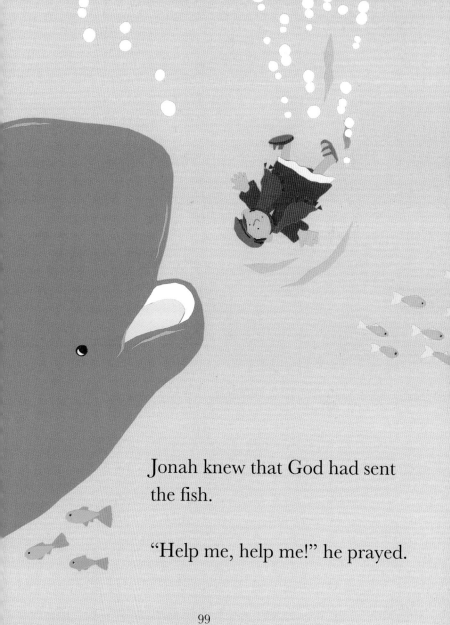

Jonah knew that God had sent
the fish.

"Help me, help me!" he prayed.

The fish spat Jonah onto dry land.

Once again God told Jonah to go to Nineveh. At last he went.

"Here is a message from God!" he cried. "Stop doing bad things. If yo don't, terrible things will happen."

The king heard the news.

"Everyone, stop being bad," he ordered.

God forgave everyone. That made Jonah very grumpy indeed.

He went and made himself a little shelter.
He sat in it and sulked.

"Why are you cross?" asked God.

"The people of Nineveh did bad things,"
said Jonah. "You shouldn't have been
kind to them."

God made a lovely plant grow
over Jonah's shelter.

It gave cool shade.

The next day, God sent a worm to eat the plant, and it died.

The sun was hot. The wind was hotter. Jonah was grumpier than ever.

"Why are you cross?" asked God. "I'm cross about my poor plant," said Jonah.

"Are you feeling sorry for a plant?" said God. "Well, I'm feeling sorry for all the people of Nineveh and all their animals. Even if they were once bad, I still love them."

Daniel and
the Lions

Daniel always did what he believed was right.

He always said prayers to God.

He always obeyed God.

Daniel did what he believed was right even when everything else went wrong.

One sad day, the great-great-great-ever-so-many-great-grandchildren of Abraham lost a fight against enemy soldiers.

Daniel was one of the people taken far away. He went to Babylon.

Everything was going wrong.

Daniel went on doing what
he believed was right.

He always followed God's laws.

The king of Babylon saw that Daniel was a good man. He gave him a very important job.

That made other people very jealous.

They went to see the king.

"O king," they said. "You are so great and wonderful. Make a law that says you will punish anyone who treats anyone else as more important than you."

"Good idea," said the king.

"Say that anyone who disobeys will be thrown into a pit of lions," said the men.

"Good idea," said the king.

Daniel knew that everything was going wrong.

He still did what he believed was right. He still said prayers to God. He still obeyed God.

The men came to spy on him. They saw what he was doing.

Then they went and told the king.

"Daniel is praying to his God. He thinks his God is greater than you."

The king was sad. Now he must punish Daniel.

Daniel was thrown
into a pit of hungry
lions.

Everything was going wrong.

Daniel still did what he believed
was right.

He still said prayers to God.

He still obeyed God.

The next morning, the king came to see what had happened.

Daniel was alive. God had not let the lions hurt him.

"Hooray!" said the king. "I shall make a law that everyone must respect Daniel's God. He will be safe, and those bad men will be punished."

Everything was going right, and Daniel still did what he believed was right.

Nehemiah's Prayers

Nehemiah worked in the palace of the emperor of Persia. One day he was feeling sad.

"Why do you look so sad?" asked the emperor.

Nehemiah said a prayer to God. Then he answered, "My real homeland is far away. Our great city was knocked down in a fight. Now that the fight is over, my people want to go back and build it up."

The emperor let Nehemiah go to help mend the city— the great city of Jerusalem, in the homeland of the great-great-great-ever-so-many-great-grandchildren of Abraham.

Nehemiah rode around the city on a donkey, looking at the broken walls.

Then he met with all the people.

"God has helped me get here," he said.
"I want to help mend the city."

"Let's all mend it,"
the people said.

Everybody worked,
and the walls began
to grow…

and grow…

Some other people came
to watch. "You'll never
mend a city as
broken down as
this," they laughed.

Nehemiah said a prayer to God. Then he
spoke to the people. "Don't worry about
what others think," he said.

Next Nehemiah heard that some people were planning to spoil all the work.

"Don't be afraid," said Nehemiah. "God will help us."

He told half the people to keep on building. The other half kept watch with swords and spears—they were ready to protect the builders.

At last the work was done. Everyone came to a great meeting.

A priest read out the laws God had given Moses: "Love God most of all, and love others as you love yourself."

Then everyone said a prayer:

"God, you made the world.
You chose Abraham to be the
great-grandfather of our people.
You chose Moses to lead us to freedom.
You took us to a homeland.
You gave us good laws.
We have sometimes disobeyed you
and made everything go wrong.
We are sorry, and we promise now
to keep your laws."

Nehemiah was happy. God had
answered all his prayers.

Tell me the stories of Jesus
   I love to hear;
things I would ask him to tell
   me if he were here;
scenes by the wayside, tales
   of the sea,
stories of Jesus, tell them to me.

A children's hymn

Baby Jesus

In the little town of Nazareth lived a young woman named Mary. She was looking forward to getting married.

One day, an angel came to visit her.

"Don't be afraid," said the angel.

"God has chosen you for
something very special.
You are going to have a baby:
God's own Son. You must call
him Jesus. He will bring God's
blessings to the world."

Mary was very surprised but she agreed.
"I will do as God wants," she said.

Mary was looking forward to
marrying Joseph. But when
Joseph heard Mary's news,
he was worried.

Then an angel spoke to him
in a dream. "Take care of
Mary," said the angel.
"Her baby is God's own
Son. He will bring God's
blessings to all the world."

Joseph was very puzzled, but he said he
would take care of Mary.

And together they went to
take part in a great counting
of people that was being done.
They went to Bethlehem.

The town was very busy.
The only place to stay
was in a room full of
animals.

There, Mary's baby was born.
Mary wrapped him in swaddling clothes.
She laid him to sleep in a manger.

Out in the fields nearby, shepherds were watching their sheep. An angel appeared.

"Do not be afraid," said the angel. "Tonight, in Bethlehem, a baby has been born: God's special king, who will bring God's blessings to the world."

Then all the angels sang together
for joy.

The shepherds went to Bethlehem.

They found Mary and the baby,
just as the angel had said.

Far away, wise men saw a special star in the night sky.

"It is a sign that a new king has been born," they said. "We must go and find him."

The star led them to the place
where Jesus was.

They brought him gifts: gold,
frankincense and myrrh.

Mary smiled. The gifts for Jesus were gifts for a king.

"The king who will bring God's blessings to the world," she said to herself.

143

Jesus Grows Up

Jesus grew up in Nazareth.

He learned the old stories: about Noah and Abraham and many others.

He learned about Moses and the
laws God had given him: "Love God
most of all, and love others as you love
yourself."

Every year, the people remembered the story of Moses and the great escape from Egypt. They held a special festival called Passover.

The best place to be at festival time was the big city of Jerusalem. When Jesus was twelve, he went with Mary and Joseph and lots of people from Nazareth.

The most important part of the festival took place in the Temple.

All around, wise teachers sat and talked
about the old stories and the laws God
had given Moses.

After the festival, everyone from
Nazareth set off for home.

They had gone some way when Mary
thought, "Where is Jesus? I haven't seen him
all day."

No one had seen him.

Mary and Joseph rushed back
to Jerusalem.

At last they found Jesus.
He was sitting with the wise
teachers, talking about the old
stories and the laws.

"Why are you here?" asked
Mary. "We have been so
worried about you."

"Why?" said Jesus. "Didn't
you know that I had to be in
my Father's house?"

Mary didn't really understand.
She just wanted Jesus to be safe.

Then Jesus went back home. He grew
to be a man. He was a good son to his
parents. He learned
the kind of work
that Joseph did.

Then, one day, he went off to
begin a new kind of work.

Jesus became a wise teacher.
He helped people understand
the old stories and the laws.
He wanted people to
understand what God
is like.

He wanted people to know
how much God loves them.

Jesus and His Friends

J esus the wise teacher told people about God. He told people that God loves them and welcomes them as friends.

"Follow me," said Jesus. "Come and listen to what I have to say, and help spread the news."

"We will come," said the fishermen. They left their fishing nets and their boat. They followed Jesus.

"I will come," said the tax collector. He left his money and his greedy friends to follow Jesus.

"I will come," said the rich lady, "for he is showing people the loving way to live, and I want to help."

There were other women, too,
who followed Jesus: some rich
and some poor.

"We will follow Jesus," said the mother and the father, "for our little girl was dead…"

"But Jesus made me as alive as can be," danced the little girl.

Other people danced too:
people who had not been able to
walk until Jesus made them well.

The sparrows twittered happily in the olive trees.

They swooped close to Jesus.

They dared to hop near his feet.

Something seemed to tell them
that Jesus noticed them and loved
them as well.

Some mothers came to Jesus. "We want Jesus to say a prayer for our children," they said.

"Sorry," said some of his
friends. "He's too busy."

"I am not too busy," said Jesus. "I welcome children. For God welcomes children.

"So all of my friends must
welcome little children and
love them."

The Hole in the Roof

Many people came to see Jesus and to listen to what he had to say. Some of the people were teachers. They were not all sure that they liked Jesus' teaching.

One day, Jesus was talking to
people inside a house.
It was very crowded.

Yet more people
came to see Jesus.

"We have heard he can heal people by
miracles," they said. "Our friend cannot
walk. We are carrying him here on his
sleeping mat so Jesus
can heal him."

There was a problem:
they could not even get into
the house.

On the outside of the house,
steps led up to the flat roof.

The men took their friend
up onto the roof.

They made a hole in the roof and
let the man down on ropes,

right in front of Jesus.

"All the bad that is in you has been forgiven," said Jesus with a smile.

"He can't say that!" said some of
the wise teachers to each other.
"Only God can say that."

Jesus smiled. He wanted people to understand that God loves people, that God forgives people, that God wants to make people well, and that God wants to be friends with people.

He said to the man,
"Get up and walk."

The man got up and walked
home. He even carried his
sleeping mat.

"God has done wonderful things
for me," he said to his friends.

The Boat in the Storm

Jesus was very busy. There always seemed to be a lot of people wanting to see him.

One evening, he said to his close friends,
"Come, let's go in our boat across to the
other side of the lake."

His friends got into the boat with him.

In the boat, Jesus soon fell
asleep.

Suddenly a strong wind began
to blow.

The waves began to crash against
the sides of the boat.

The waves began to
spill into the boat.

184

"Wake up and help us," shouted Jesus' friends. "We are going to sink with the boat!"

Jesus stood up.

"Be quiet," he said to the waves.
"Be still," he said to the wind.

Then everything was calm.
Everything that was dark and
dangerous and scary just went
away.

The day came, bright and clear.

"What made you so scared?" asked
Jesus. "Don't you believe in God?"

Jesus' friends knew they were safe,
but they were more scared than ever.

"Who is our friend Jesus?" they
asked each other. "Who can he be?
Even the wind and waves obey him."

The Good Samaritan

A teacher once came
and asked Jesus a question:
"What is the right way
to live?"

Jesus asked him a question:
"You are a teacher. What
do the old stories and the
laws say?"

"Love God most of all, and love
others as you love yourself,"
answered the man.

"You are right," said Jesus.
"You know what to do."

"But who are these 'others'?"
asked the man.

Jesus told a story.

"Once there was a man who went on a journey.

"On the way, robbers attacked him. They took everything he had and beat him up.

"They left him lying in the road.

"A priest from the Temple
came along.

"He saw the man, but hurried on
by on the other side of the road.

"A helper from the Temple
came along.

"He came and looked
at the man. Then he hurried
on by.

"A Samaritan came along."

"Samaritans are no good," said
someone listening. "They don't
like us, and we don't like them."

Jesus went on with the story:
"The Samaritan saw the man.
He stopped. He bandaged the
man's cuts.

"Then he lifted the man onto his donkey and took him to an inn.

"He gave the innkeeper some money. 'Take care of him till I come back,' he said. 'If you need to spend more, I'll pay the extra.'"

Then Jesus asked the teacher a question: "Who showed the right way to love others?"

"The one who was kind," answered the teacher.

Jesus said, "You go, then, and
do the same."

The Lost Sheep

J esus welcomed all kinds
of people: he didn't seem
to mind what sort of people
they were.

Some had become rich
by cheating.

Some lived bad lives.

Some had the kinds of diseases that no one else wanted to get near.

The teachers were surprised. "What sort of person is Jesus if he wants to be friends with them?" they wondered.

Jesus told a story.

"Imagine that you have a hundred sheep. You take good care of them.

"One day when you are
counting them, you find that
one is missing.

"Where can it be?
What are you going to do?

207

"You leave the other ninety-nine nibbling in the pasture.

"You go looking for the one
that is lost.

"You look high…

and low…

and everywhere in between…

"When you find it, you are so happy you pick it up and carry it home.

"You call out to your friends,
'Come and celebrate with me!
I had lost this sheep, but I have
found it again!'

"God is like that shepherd," said Jesus. "God sees the people who live good lives. God also sees those who have wandered away from what is good—and God cares about them too.

"There is more happiness in
heaven when one is found and
brought back home than over
ninety-nine that are already safe."

A Prayer for Always

Jesus liked to pray to God.

Sometimes he went into a room by himself and closed the door. There, alone and quietly, he prayed to God.

Sometimes he got up early and
went for a walk in the hills.
There, alone and quietly, he
prayed to God.

"Teach us to pray," his friends
asked him.

"Here is a prayer for always,"
said Jesus.

"Father in heaven:
May your name be kept holy.
May your Kingdom come
and may your will be done
on earth as it is in heaven."

"I know what that means," said
one of the friends.
"God is our kind father. We want
people to obey God so the whole
world is as good
as heaven."

"Next," said Jesus, "say this:

"Give us today the food
we need."

"Oh good, I don't like being
hungry," said one.

"Food makes the body strong,"
said another, "but we also need
God to encourage us, to make us
strong inside."

That made everyone think.

"Ask God this," said Jesus.

"Forgive us the wrongs we have done, as we forgive the wrongs that others have done to us."

"Do we always have to forgive everyone?"
asked the friend called Peter.
"I try, but some people go on doing bad
things."

"You must forgive everyone over and
over again," said Jesus.

"Then," said Jesus, "say this:

"Do not bring us to hard testing, but keep us safe from the Evil One."

Everyone looked a bit sad.

"Do hard things happen to people who live as God wants?" someone asked.

Jesus sighed and nodded. He knew there were hard times ahead.

"But God is God forever and ever," another replied.

And that made everyone glad.

Almost
the End

It was a day in spring, on the road to Jerusalem.

Many people were going to celebrate the Passover festival at the Temple there.

Jesus came along, riding on a donkey.

The crowds welcomed him like a king.

They waved palm branches and cheered. "This must be the beginning of Jesus making the whole world a better place," they said to each other.

Jesus went to the Temple. It was like a marketplace. People were selling the things people needed to buy for the festival.

Jesus could see that they were making people pay too much.

Suddenly he began upsetting the
whole market.

"How dare you!" shouted the people in charge
of the Temple.

"The Temple is meant to be a place where you pray," said Jesus. "Not a place where people are cheated."

The people in charge were very angry.

"We must get rid of Jesus," they whispered. They began to make a plan.

A few days later, Jesus met with his friends
to eat the festival meal.

He warned them of hard times ahead.

He told them always to love one another.

He shared bread and wine with them. He told
them always to share bread and wine and to
remember him in this special way.

Then Jesus went out to
a quiet place to pray.

"Father God," he said,
"I don't want these hard times,
but I will do what
you want."

Already one of Jesus' friends had joined the plan to get rid of Jesus.

He came with soldiers who took Jesus away.

The next day, Jesus was put to death, nailed to a cross of wood.

In the evening, a few friends came and took the body to a tomb.

"We must say goodbye," said one.

The sky was getting dark. "This must be the end of Jesus making the world a better place," they wept.

Good News

It was the weekly day of rest.
Jesus' friends were very sad,
for Jesus was dead.

"We'll have to hide," said some. "We might get into trouble for being his friends."

"But we will go back to the tomb," said the women, "to say goodbye properly."

The next morning, very early,
the women went. To their surprise,
the tomb was open.

Inside were two angels in shining white
clothes. "Jesus is not here,"
they said. "He is alive."

They ran to tell the others, but no
one really believed them.

That evening, two of
Jesus' friends left
Jerusalem for home.
A man was going the
same way. As they
walked, they talked
about Jesus.

"Stay with us," said the two friends when
they reached home.

When they began the meal, the man said
the mealtime prayer and broke the bread to
share it.

The two friends gasped. It was Jesus.
But all at once he was gone.

Other friends saw Jesus.

He shared a meal with them.

He helped them understand that
God is a friend when people face
hard times, and that God can make
everything good and right again.

He gave them a job to do—to tell this
news to all the world.

Soon after, Jesus went to heaven.

But God gave his friends the help they needed.

They suddenly felt brave.
They knew what to say.

They began to speak to anyone
who would listen.

"Jesus came to us from God," they explained.

"He came to tell us how much God loves us. People tried to stop him, but their plan hasn't worked.

"Jesus is alive, proving that his message is true: God wants everyone to give up bad ways and come home to a place of goodness. God welcomes us all as friends.

"That's everyone in the whole wide world forever."

The news has been spreading ever since.

Index

When you look up the pages in this list, remember to read the whole story to find out more.